T is for Tortilla

Text © Jody Alpers 2005
Illustrations © Celeste Johnson 2005

ISBN 13: 978-1-929115-14-3
ISBN 10: 1-929115-14-8
Library of Congress Control Number: 2005938527

Primary text: Futura 14 pts.
Additional text: Toddler 18 pts. and Bermuda drop caps, 40 pts.

Book design by Maureen Burdock, THEMA

Printed in Canada
by Friesens Corporation

Azro Press
PMB 342 • 1704 B Llano Street
Santa Fe, NM 87505
www.azropress.com

T is for Tortilla

A Southwestern Alphabet Book

Written by Jody Alpers

Illustrated by Celeste Johnson

To Greg, the love of my life.
In memory of SueSue Forbes (1947-2006)
my sister and first publisher. JA

Dedicated to the glory of God
and to my daughters Cristina and Tiffany.
Your love and support mean so much.
I love you.
And in memory of my mom (1914-2005). CJ

A is for Adobe

Have you ever heard of a house made of mud? Adobe is made by mixing mud and straw. The mud is poured into molds to be dried in the sun. The adobe bricks are used to build buildings and walls. Would you like to live in a house made of mud?

B is for Balloon

Would you like to ride on the wind?
You can in a hot air balloon. A big basket is
attached to a giant colorful balloon. The balloon
is filled with hot air and it slowly floats high up
in the sky. The balloon moves with the wind.
There are balloon fiestas all
over the Southwest.

C is for cowboy

In the Southwest there are many ranches where cattle are raised. Cowboys take care of the cattle. They ride horses and wear cowboy boots and hats. Do you see some other pictures on this page that have the same beginning sound as cowboy?

D is for Desert

A desert is a place where it doesn't rain much. It is so dry not many plants and animals can live in the desert. Cacti live in the desert. Can you see some other plants and animals that live in the desert?

E is for Ewe

A ewe is a mother sheep. Some ranches in
the Southwest raise sheep instead of cattle.
Sheep are raised for their meat and wool.
How many ewes have baby lambs
in this picture?

F is for Fiesta

Fiesta is a Spanish word for a party or celebration. Usually a band plays and people dance. Sometimes people play games and eat great food. Maybe you could call your next party a fiesta.

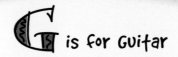 **G** is for Guitar

A guitar is a musical instrument with a curved body and a long neck. It has six strings that are strummed or plucked. People often sing and play the guitar at the same time. Have you ever played a guitar?

H is for Hacienda

Hacienda is a Spanish word for a ranch house. A hacienda is usually very large. There is a song called "My Adobe Hacienda." Can you guess what the house in the song was made of?

I is for Indian culture

There are different tribes of American Indians in the Southwest. Indian food, art, music, and language are all part of Southwest culture today. This picture shows an Indian woman weaving a rug.

J is for Jackrabbit

A jackrabbit has long ears and can run fast. The blacktail jackrabbit is the most common in the Southwest. Its coat is mostly grey flecked with black. Its ears are 6 or 7 inches long!

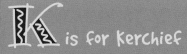 **is for kerchief**

A Cowboy wears a kerchief around his neck to keep off the sun. Sometimes he pulls it up over his nose to keep from breathing too much dust. You can make your own cowboy kerchief by folding a square scarf or bandana into a triangle and tying it over your nose.

L is for Luminarias

Luminarias are Christmas decorations used in the Southwest. They are brown paper sacks filled half way with sand. A small candle is placed inside each one. The sacks are lined up on roofs, walls, or walkways. When the candles are lit, the luminarias make a beautiful decoration. The tradition says the candles light the way for the Christ Child. In northern New Mexico luminarias are called farolitos.

M is for Mesa

A mesa is a mountain that is different from any other type of mountain because it is flat on top with steep rock sides. Some people call this a tabletop mountain. Would you like to try to climb a mesa? Do you think it would be easy?

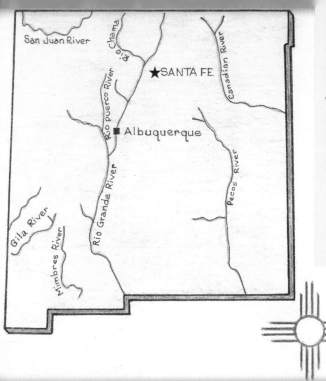

New Mexico is the 47th state. Some people think New Mexico is in Old Mexico and do not know it is in the United States, but it is. New Mexico is the fifth largest state.

O is for ollas

Ollas are Indian water pots. The Pueblo Indians used to keep their drinking water in these pots. They did not move around like the Plains Indians did so they could have many big clay pots and bowls. Why do you think the Plains Indians did not have many ollas?

P is for Piñata

A piñata is used for parties or fiestas. It is a paper-mâché figure covered with brightly colored tissue paper. The middle of it is filled with candy. Children take turns hitting the piñata with a stick. When the piñata breaks, all the children scramble to get the candy. Do you think it would be fun to try to break a piñata?

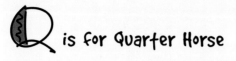 **is for Quarter Horse**

Many cowboys of the Southwest ride quarter horses. The quarter horse got his name because he is fast in the quarter-mile race. He is also strong, quick, and can turn fast. He helps the cowboy work with cattle.

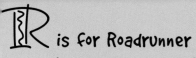

R is for Roadrunner

A roadrunner is a type of bird found in the Southwest. He would rather run than fly. The roadrunner's favorite foods are mice and rattlesnakes. People in the Southwest like it when a roadrunner lives near their house. Can you guess why?

S is for Sunset

The Southwest is known for its beautiful sunsets.
As the sun goes down in the evening, you can see many
pretty colors. This is called a sunset. People think the sunsets in the
Southwest are the most beautiful in the world. Can you name some of the
colors in this picture of a sunset?

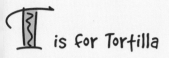 is for Tortilla

A tortilla is a type of bread. It does not come in a loaf like other bread. It is flat and round and cooked on both sides. Tortillas can be made from flour or corn. They are used in many Mexican dishes or eaten plain. Have you ever eaten a tortilla?

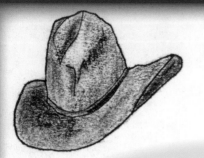

𝒰 is for Uno

Uno is the Spanish word for the number one. Can you count how many things on these pages have uno?

V is for Viga

A viga is a long log used to hold up a roof or ceiling in an adobe house. Sometimes a viga is so long that it sticks out to the outside of a house. How many vigas do you see in this ceiling?

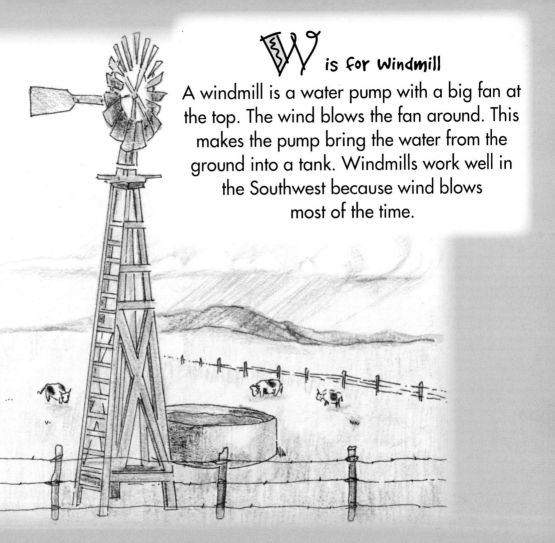

W is for Windmill

A windmill is a water pump with a big fan at the top. The wind blows the fan around. This makes the pump bring the water from the ground into a tank. Windmills work well in the Southwest because wind blows most of the time.

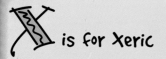

X is for Xeric

Many plants in the Southwest are xeric. Xeric means the plants grow best in dry weather. These pages show some plants that are xeric.

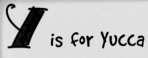

Y is for Yucca

A yucca is one type of xeric plant. It likes dry heat.
Instead of having leaves, this plant has sharp spines.
It has pretty yellow flowers. Can you guess how this
plant got the nickname "the Spanish Sword"?

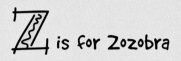 is for Zozobra

Zozobra* is a 49-foot high puppet made of wood, cloth, and wire. It is stuffed with shredded paper. The puppet is also known as Old Man Gloom. He moves his arms, his head, and his mouth. At a big fiesta in Santa Fe every September, Zozobra is burned to drive away gloom in the coming year.

Before Zozobra is set on fire, a fire dancer and children dressed as "glooms" dance in front of him and make him mad. Zozobra moans and groans. Zozobra burns to the ground, and all our troubles go up in smoke.

Pronunciation Guide

This alphabet book tells about many things found in the Southwest. Some of the words in the book are Spanish or Indian words so we have made "helper words" to help you learn how to say them. Have fun learning new alphabet words from the Southwest!

Adobe (ah-DOH-bey)
Balloon
Cowboy
Desert
Ewe (you)
Farolito (fa-roh-LEE-to)
Fiesta (fee-YES-tah)
Guitar
Hacienda (ah-see-EN-dah)
Indian Culture
Jackrabbit
Kerchief
Luminaria (loo-mee-NAHR-ee-ah)
Mesa (MAY-sah)

New Mexico
Ollas (OY-yahs)
Piñata (peen-NYA-tah)
Quarter Horse
Roadrunner
Sunset
Tortilla (tor-TEE-yah)
Uno (OO-no)
Vigas (VEE-gahs)
Windmill
Xeric (Zee-rik)
Yucca (YUK-ah)
Zozobra™(zo-ZO-brah)